Aladdin and the Wonderful Lamp

A Pantomime in Three Acts

K. O. Samuel

A Samuel French Acting Edition

SAMUELFRENCH-LONDON.CO.UK
SAMUELFRENCH.COM

Copyright © 1930 by Samuel French Ltd
All Rights Reserved

ALADDIN AND THE WONDERFUL LAMP is fully protected under the copyright laws of the British Commonwealth, including Canada, the United States of America, and all other countries of the Copyright Union. All rights, including professional and amateur stage productions, recitation, lecturing, public reading, motion picture, radio broadcasting, television and the rights of translation into foreign languages are strictly reserved.

ISBN 978-0-573-06405-0

www.samuelfrench-london.co.uk

www.samuelfrench.com

For Amateur Production Enquiries

United Kingdom and World excluding North America

plays@SamuelFrench-London.co.uk

020 7255 4302/01

Each title is subject to availability from Samuel French,

depending upon country of performance.

CAUTION: Professional and amateur producers are hereby warned that ALADDIN AND THE WONDERFUL LAMP is subject to a licensing fee. Publication of this play does not imply availability for performance. Both amateurs and professionals considering a production are strongly advised to apply to the appropriate agent before starting rehearsals, advertising, or booking a theatre. A licensing fee must be paid whether the title is presented for charity or gain and whether or not admission is charged.

The professional rights in this play are controlled by Samuel French Ltd, 52 Fitzroy Street, London, W1T 5JR.

No one shall make any changes in this title for the purpose of production. No part of this book may be reproduced, stored in a retrieval system, or transmitted in any form, by any means, now known or yet to be invented, including mechanical, electronic, photocopying, recording, videotaping, or otherwise, without the prior written permission of the publisher. No one shall upload this title, or part of this title, to any social media websites.

The right of K. O. Samuel to be identified as author of this work has been asserted by him in accordance with Section 77 of the Copyright, Designs and Patents Act 1988

CAST

ALADDIN.
WIDOW TWANKEY.
SING-SING (a Chinaman).
THE AFRICAN MAGICIAN.
THE EMPEROR OF CHINA.
BALDROUBADOUR (his Daughter).
ESMERALDA (her Maid).
MUSTAPHA (the Grand Vizier).
SLAVE OF THE RING.
SLAVE OF THE LAMP.
Chorus of Chinese girls, Courtiers, Attendants, etc.

SCENES

ACT I
A Street in Peking.

ACT II
SCENE 1.—Outside the Cave.
SCENE 2.—Inside the Cave.
SCENE 3.—Twankey's Home.

ACT III
SCENE 1.—Aladdin's Palace.
SCENE 2.—The same.

Published songs, opening choruses, finales and incidental music suitable for the purpose of interspersing the dialogue of this pantomime can be easily procured through a local music store.

ALADDIN AND THE WONDERFUL LAMP

ACT I

SCENE.—*A Street in Peking.*

(WIDOW TWANKEY'S *shop down* R. CURTAIN *rises on Opening Chorus of Chinese girls. During the final bars of the chorus,* WIDOW TWANKEY *pokes her head through the shop window.*)

WIDOW TWANKEY. That's right, girls, enjoy yourselves. I'll be with you in a minute. (*She skips through the doorway and dances round the stage.*) Keep it up, my dears. I must have my constitootional. This is the way to start the day. Keep that schoolgirl complexion, clear away those crow's-feet and come to Peking, it's so bracing.

(*Music stops.*)

There! Now we're all ready for the day's work. Ladies, can I show you anything this morning?

CHORUS. No, thanks.

WIDOW TWANKEY. Eh? Oh! Would any of you like to step in and have a look round?

CHORUS. No, thanks.

WIDOW TWANKEY. Well, can I bring anything out and show it to you?

CHORUS. No, thanks.

WIDOW TWANKEY. Can I send you any samples on appro?

CHORUS. No, thanks.

WIDOW TWANKEY. But, ladies, don't you realize

6 ALADDIN AND THE WONDERFUL LAMP.

there's a sale on ?—That the stock simply *must* be cleared ?—that everything is being disposed of regardless of cost ?—that——
Chorus. We haven't got any money.
Widow Twankey. Eh?
Chorus (*shouting*). We haven't got any money.
Widow Twankey. Well, why didn't you say so before? Go inside, my dears, and help yourselves.

(Chorus *crowd into the shop*.)

Widow Twankey (*to audience*). There you are, that's the sort of silly thing I do. I shall never make this business pay. I'm much too kind. To tell you the truth, I don't like these Eastern methods. You see, I'm not Chinese really. Oh dear no! I'm London all over—Barking. And no woman's going to call herself a Pekingese if she's Barking. Old Twankey, you know, was such a restless chap—always on the move, trying to find a nice place to settle down—like a bluebottle looking for a piece of meat. But I'm not grumbling. Peking suits me, and now I've got the Air Service I'm in touch with Barking in no time. The non-stop flight's worth doing any week-end, you know. Leaving Peking Saturday afternoon, having tea with the Vicar of Barking on Sunday and getting back in time to make the chop-suey of a Monday morning.

Song : Widow Twankey.

(*Enter* Sing-Sing l., *a benevolent-looking Chinaman, wearing large horn-rimmed glasses and carrying a badly rolled umbrella. He walks on jauntily, singing the last bars of the Opening Chorus, and catches sight of* Widow Twankey.)

Sing-Sing. Ah, Mrs. Twankey, I *thought* I should find you in.
Widow Twankey. I'm not in. I'm out.
Sing-Sing (*wagging his umbrella at her playfully*). Now, now, Mrs. Twankey, no stories! I can see you!
Widow Twankey. Yes, but I'm not in. (*Points

ALADDIN AND THE WONDERFUL LAMP.

to shop.) That's "in." This is "out." I'm not *in*, so I'm *out*.

SING-SING. No, no, Mrs. Twankey, don't muddle me. Now you've driven everything out of my head. (*Scratches head.*)

WIDOW TWANKEY. Then there's no need to scratch it.

SING-SING (*nervously*). Mrs. Twankey—ever since I first met you—er—that is to say—when I first saw you—I mean—as soon as I looked at you for the first time—I said to myself, "How wonderfully you"—that is—er—how—how— (*in a feeble attempt to gain time*) how are you?

WIDOW TWANKEY. I'm quite well, thank you.

SING-SING. Yes, that's it—quite well. You *are* quite well, you are wonderful, you are—— (*With sudden resolution.*) Mrs. Twankey, I——

WIDOW TWANKEY. Mr. Sing, I think you might have waited until the last Act before proposing to me.

SING-SING. But I *haven't* proposed yet!

WIDOW TWANKEY. No, but I can feel it coming up. Does this umbrella open? (*Takes his umbrella.*) Because if it does, I should like to hide my blushes. (*Opens umbrella.*)

SING-SING. Mrs. Twankey, don't do that. It's unlucky.

WIDOW TWANKEY. Well, you'll be unlucky in any case, so it doesn't matter.

SING-SING. Am I refused, Mrs. Twankey? Am I repulsed?

WIDOW TWANKEY. Even so, Mr. Sing.

SING-SING (*preparing to go*). Then, I shall throw myself into the river.

WIDOW TWANKEY. In that case you'd better take the umbrella. (*Gives him the umbrella. He moves off dejectedly.*) Mr. Sing. (*He turns to her.*) Before you throw yourself into the river, I think I ought to tell you that I was only teasing.

SING-SING. Teasing?

WIDOW TWANKEY (*coyly*). Yes, I love to play with men. What are your prospects, Mr. Sing?

SING-SING. You have heard of my business in Peking. Sing-Sing the Great Tailor.

WIDOW TWANKEY. I couldn't marry a tailor, he would be full of pins. But, to come to the point, do you realize that I have a son, Aladdin, and that you would have to take him on as well?

SING-SING. There is room for him in the business.

WIDOW TWANKEY. You don't know my Aladdin. He's such a mischievous young scamp. I can do nothing with him.

(ALADDIN *calls off stage:* "Mother! Mother!")

That's him. Always shouting "Mother, Mother" up and down the streets and spoiling my chances.

(ALADDIN *runs on* L.)

ALADDIN. Mother, what do you think? I've just won ten bob at Crown and Anchor. Now we can go and have an expensive lunch.

(ALADDIN *catches sight of* SING-SING.)

Hullo, what's this?

SING-SING (*annoyed*). You mean "*Who's* this?"

WIDOW TWANKEY. Aladdin, this is Mr. Sing-Sing.

ALADDIN. Cheerio, Ching Ching. (*Shakes his hand vigorously.*) Have a sweet? (*Offers bag of sweets.*)

SING-SING. No, thanks, I don't eat sweets.

ALADDIN. Mother, why is he called Sing-Sing—twice—like that?

WIDOW TWANKEY. Because it's his name, stupid.

ALADDIN. Oh, I see. Christian name "Sing," surname—er—"Sing."

WIDOW TWANKEY. Aladdin, Mr. Sing-Sing says he has room for you in his business.

ALADDIN. Then tell him to mind his own business.

WIDOW TWANKEY (*to* SING-SING). There you are, you see what a charming son I have.

ALADDIN. Mother, I saw the Princess just now, on her way to the bath. She looked fine. I should like to marry her.

ALADDIN AND THE WONDERFUL LAMP.

SING-SING (*sneering*). Perhaps you will, some day. (*Laughs.*)

ALADDIN (*pugnaciously*). I don't see anything to laugh at. Anyway, I'm not going into a common business. I'm going to do big things and astonish the world. I don't quite know how, though. I haven't thought it out yet.

WIDOW TWANKEY. You'd better think it out now, then. Can I offer you a little refreshment, Mr. Sing ?

(*They move towards the shop.*)

SING-SING. I don't drink at this time of the morning, Mrs. Twankey, but I think perhaps a plate of rice——

WIDOW TWANKEY. Ah, you are very clever, Mr. Sing.

SING-SING. Clever, Mrs. Twankey ?

WIDOW TWANKEY. They always throw *rice* at the bride where I come from, Mr. Sing. (*Giggles affectedly.*)

(*They go into shop.*)

ALADDIN. How beautiful the Princess was ! I shall wait until she comes back from the bath. She comes this way, too. What can I do to attract her attention ? Sing to her ? Yes, princesses are always fond of music. What shall I sing ? I know.

SONG : ALADDIN.

(*Exit* L. *after song.*)

(*The* MAGICIAN *enters up* R., *creeping on with dramatic caution.*)

MAGICIAN. This must be the street. Now, which way did that youngster go, I wonder ? But stay ! Perhaps he lives here. I will investigate. (*Creeps round and peers into the shop window.*)

(ALADDIN *enters* L., *eating an apple. He sees the* MAGICIAN, *whose back is turned.* ALADDIN *throws the apple at him.* MAGICIAN *turns round with a snarl, drawing his knife.*)

(*Recognizing* ALADDIN.) It's the boy himself. (*He puts*

10 ALADDIN AND THE WONDERFUL LAMP.

his knife away. His expression changes and he advances with a cunning smile towards ALADDIN, *who is about to run off in a fright.*) Don't be alarmed, my boy. I won't hurt you.

ALADDIN. You—you frightened me for the moment. What was the idea of all that creepy-crawly stuff?

(MAGICIAN *gives a quick look round and then takes* ALADDIN *down stage to* C.)

MAGICIAN. What is your name, boy?

ALADDIN. Aladdin.

MAGICIAN (*mysteriously*). Prepare yourself for some interesting news. I am your long-lost uncle.

ALADDIN. I didn't know I had one to lose.

MAGICIAN. Has your mother never told you that her husband had a brother?

ALADDIN. I've heard mother speak of Uncle sometimes. But he's not a bit like you. He lives at the pawnshop.

MAGICIAN. Aladdin, embrace your real uncle.

ALADDIN. But how do I know you *are* my uncle? Let me see. What do long-lost uncles usually do when they discover their nephews? (*Thinks.*) I know! They give them a nice bright new half-crown. (*Holds out his hand.*) Have you got a nice bright new half-crown?

MAGICIAN (*bringing out a purse*). Take this purse, Aladdin, and look inside.

ALADDIN (*giving a gasp*). Why, it's full of gold!

MAGICIAN. A little present for you.

ALADDIN. Oooo—I say! I think you really must be my uncle. (*Embraces* MAGICIAN.) Come on, nunky, let's go and blow it on cream doughnuts.

MAGICIAN. I'm too old for cream doughnuts, my boy.

ALADDIN. Good. There'll be all the more for me. I suppose *you* eat digestive biscuits or something? Let's see how much there is. (*He examines the purse.*)

MAGICIAN (*aside*). This lad will suit me well. I will use his love of gold to accomplish my purpose.

ALADDIN AND THE WONDERFUL LAMP. 11

ALADDIN. I say, nunky, how many doughnuts can you buy for that? (*Holds up coin.*)

MAGICIAN. I should say quite enough to give you a pain in the tummy.

(ALADDIN *goes into roars of laughter.* MAGICIAN *joins in.*)

ALADDIN. I bet you I can eat a dozen without getting my ears wet.

(*They go off together up* R. *arm-in-arm.*)

(WIDOW TWANKEY *and* SING-SING *come out of the shop.*)

WIDOW TWANKEY. Now you really *must* go, you naughty man. I don't know what the neighbours would say, Mr. Sing, if they knew I'd had such a bold young man in the house—and given him rice too.

SING-SING. It was very nice rice. At my lodgings they always make it so lumpy, and when I complain, they say I've got to lump it. But how can I lump it when it's lumpy already?

(CHORUS *cheering off stage.*)

Are they cheering us, do you think, Mrs. Twankey?

WIDOW TWANKEY. That's for the Princess, silly. She passes along here on her way from the bath.

SING-SING. I'm not interested, Mrs. Twankey. For me, there is only one Princess.

(*He kisses her hand sloppily and exits up* R. WIDOW TWANKEY *looks coy. Music for Princess's entrance.* CHORUS *enter* L., *walking backwards and bowing low.* BALDROUBADOUR *enters with* ESMERALDA, *her maid.*)

BALDROUBADOUR. I always think these people look so silly walking backwards.

ESMERALDA. They are paying tribute to your high estate, Princess.

BALDROUBADOUR. I don't see why I shouldn't be allowed to go and have my bath without so much publicity. Oh, look! What a darling little shop! And what a picturesque old woman outside!

12 ALADDIN AND THE WONDERFUL LAMP.

(WIDOW TWANKEY, *who is sitting outside her shop, is not too pleased with the doubtful compliment.*)

Shall we go and talk to her ?
ESMERALDA. It is strictly against etiquette, Princess.
BALDROUBADOUR. Not at all. Father said I was to do Welfare Work in the Slums, to give me an interest in life.

(WIDOW TWANKEY *registers annoyance at the word " slums."*)

ESMERALDA. I will prepare the woman for the honour that is to be conferred on her.

(ESMERALDA *goes to* WIDOW TWANKEY.)

ESMERALDA. The Princess Baldroubadour wishes to honour you with her notice.
WIDOW TWANKEY. Will this be reported in the Press ?
ESMERALDA. Of course.
WIDOW TWANKEY. Then I'll consent to be interviewed.

(WIDOW TWANKEY *comes forward and curtsies. Tear cloth off stage. She regards her dress anxiously.*)

BALDROUBADOUR. And what is your name ?
WIDOW TWANKEY. Twankey, your Highness.
BALDROUBADOUR (*to* ESMERALDA). A good old Chinese name. You do not look pure Chinese.
WIDOW TWANKEY. I have a dash of Europe in my blood, your Highness—Barking, to be precise. And I must confess I feel all the better for it, thank you very much.
BALDROUBADOUR. And do you manage to make both ends meet ?

(WIDOW TWANKEY *is fiddling with her apron-strings.*)

WIDOW TWANKEY. If your Highness will excuse my back, you may be able to see for yourself. (*Turns round.*) Is all well behind ? (*Business of turning slowly round, in the manner of a dress mannequin.*)

This reminds me of my young days. I was much sought after as a mannequin.

BALDROUBADOUR. I should like to see some of your latest models.

WIDOW TWANKEY. Modom shall be attended to immediately. (*Claps hands. Chorus girl comes out of shop carrying a pile of cardboard boxes.*) Thank you, my dear. Modom is perhaps thinking of—— ?

BALDROUBADOUR. Oh, just a little frock to slip on in the evenings.

WIDOW TWANKEY. Here is something quiet and effective. (*Holds up something very gaudy.*)

BALDROUBADOUR. Charming. Could I see it on?

WIDOW TWANKEY. Modom would wish me to slip it on? Certainly. Modom will find it slips on very easily.

(*Business of struggling in and out of dress. She catches her foot in it. Tear cloth.*)

That will make it easier for Modom to slip on. (*She sticks her head through a hole in the dress.*) Modom will find a choice of several openings.

BALDROUBADOUR (*laughing*). I couldn't possibly buy that. Why, it's full of holes!

WIDOW TWANKEY. Yes, it is a bit porous, isn't it? Perhaps Modom would prefer something a little less draughty. (*Opens another box.*) Here is a stylish five-o'clock tea-gown—if Modom cares for five-o'clock tea. (*Holds up a very faded gown.*)

BALDROUBADOUR. Oh, I think that's too killing.

WIDOW TWANKEY. Yes, perhaps Modom is right. It is just a little bit *too* killing. (*Throws it to her assistant.*) Put it back, my dear, before it does any more damage.

BALDROUBADOUR. Have you any wraps?

WIDOW TWANKEY. I have no ready-made wraps, but I have some very smart wrapping material. (*Brings out several yards of bright cloth.*) Modom will find this wraps very well. (*Business of wrapping the cloth round herself.*)

BALDROUBADOUR. The colour is very upsetting.

14   ALADDIN AND THE WONDERFUL LAMP.

Widow Twankey (*who is getting twisted up*). I'm afraid it's upsetting me more than you. *She has wound herself up like a mummy, trips and falls.*)

(Aladdin *enters up* R. *and comes down* C.)

Aladdin. Mummy! What are you doing?

Widow Twankey. Just wrapping myself up, my boy, like a good mummy.

(Aladdin *stops short on seeing the Princess.*)

Aladdin. Oh!——

Widow Twankey. Don't stare, my boy. It's rude. And take your hat off to the Princess.

Baldroubadour (*interested*). He's very sweet, isn't he?

Esmeralda. It is not etiquette for the Princess to look at street urchins.

Baldroubadour (*with sudden determination*). I want to talk to him. Walk on ahead. I'll catch you up.

Esmeralda. But your Royal Highness can't possibly——

Baldroubadour. I'll take the consequences. I order you to walk on ahead.

Esmeralda. Very well, your Highness. (*Looks at* Aladdin, *sniffs and walks off with her nose in the air.*)

Widow Twankey (*who has now unwrapped herself*). Modom has not yet given her orders.

Baldroubadour. Take away the boxes, distribute the contents among the girls and charge it up to me.

(*The girls excitedly pick up the boxes, pushing* Widow Twankey *towards the shop.*)

Widow Twankey (*who is being hustled*). For goodness' sake don't push. You won't get anything by pushing.

(*Girls disappear into shop, laughing and chatting.* Widow Twankey *is swept in with the tide.*)

Baldroubadour. There! That was rather clever of me, wasn't it?

ALADDIN. I expected you would do that, Princess.

BALDROUBADOUR. I think you are a very forward young man to *expect* anything.

ALADDIN. Somehow I don't seem to be a bit afraid of you.

BALDROUBADOUR. You ought to be. I am a *Princess*, and you are a——

ALADDIN. What am I, Princess?

BALDROUBADOUR. You are very—very—er—very nice, I think.

(ALADDIN *springs forward and kisses her hand. She gives a deep sigh.*)

That's as far as I ever get—having my hand kissed. Sometimes I wish I wasn't so exclusive.

ALADDIN. Try to forget it, for once.

BALDROUBADOUR. How can I do that?

ALADDIN. Think of yourself as someone very humble, —say, a typist, and imagine this is your afternoon out.

BALDROUBADOUR. Typists don't have afternoons out, do they? They have evenings off.

ALADDIN. Well, imagine you're a nursemaid, walking out with——

BALDROUBADOUR. With you in the pram?

ALADDIN. I'll be in the pram, if you promise to kiss me.

BALDROUBADOUR. No, Aladdin, that cannot be. I cannot forget that I am royal.

ALADDIN. Then think of me as royal too.

BALDROUBADOUR (*to see how it sounds*). Prince Aladdin!

ALADDIN. Prince Aladdin! Yes, that's it. Why didn't I think of it before? I'll be a Prince and you shall be my Princess.

DUET: BALDROUBADOUR *and* ALADDIN.

(*Exeunt* L. *after number.*)

(*The girls crowd out of the shop, each with a box.* WIDOW TWANKEY *appears in the doorway, waving them good-bye. Business of thanking her.* 'Thank you so

much, Mrs. Twankey, for the *lovely* present."
"Awfully kind of you to *give* it away." "You *are*
a dear," etc., etc. *They fade off in couples* L. *and up*
R.)

WIDOW TWANKEY (*coming* C.). There you are, I've
done it this time. I've cleared my stock-in-trade. I'm
a foolish woman, I know, but I've done it, and if the
Princess doesn't pay up, I shall have to throw myself on
the Parish.

(ALADDIN'S *voice heard singing off stage.*)

There's that boy giving tongue again. A fat lot he'd
care *where* I threw myself.

(*Enter* ALADDIN L., *singing and throwing his cap in the
air.*)

Don't throw that cap about, my boy. You won't get
a new one this year.

ALADDIN. Mother, this is my lucky day.

WIDOW TWANKEY. What have you been scrounging
now?

ALADDIN. I've just scrounged an uncle.

WIDOW TWANKEY. A what?——

ALADDIN. An uncle, a nice rich one. Look, he's
given me this. (*Holds up purse.*)

(WIDOW TWANKEY *snatches it and looks inside.*)

WIDOW TWANKEY (*faintly*). It's full of gold! Show
him in at once.

ALADDIN (*calling*). Come on, nunky. Come and
be introduced.

(*Enter* MAGICIAN L.)

MAGICIAN. Ah, dear sister! Behold your husband's
long-lost brother!

WIDOW TWANKEY. Ah, my dear brother-in-law!

(*They embrace.*)

ALADDIN. Introductions don't seem to be necessary.

ALADDIN AND THE WONDERFUL LAMP. 17

WIDOW TWANKEY. It is certainly strange that the late Twankey never told me he had a brother. But that was like poor old Twankey. Very secretive, he was—always hushing things up—including his wife. By the way—(*holds out purse*) you—er—haven't got any more—er—spare cash like this—sort of knocking about, I suppose?

MAGICIAN. That! Oh, that's nothing. (*Laughs disdainfully.*)

WIDOW TWANKEY. Nothing!

ALADDIN. But it's full of gold!

MAGICIAN. I have plenty like that.

ALADDIN. To *give* away?

MAGICIAN. Yes, yes, to give away.

WIDOW TWANKEY. D'you mind saying that again? (*Faintly.*) I'm not quite sure whether I heard you properly.

MAGICIAN (*going up and shouting in her ear*). I have plenty of gold to give away.

WIDOW TWANKEY (*still feeling faint*). Oh yes, there was no mistake about it that time. (*Holds her hand out.*) Put it there, brother.

MAGICIAN (*shaking hands with her vigorously*). I am made of gold.

WIDOW TWANKEY (*looking at her hand*). Yes, but it doesn't seem to come off.

(MAGICIAN *seizes their hands and drags them down stage dramatically.*)

MAGICIAN. I am going to tell you a secret.

WIDOW TWANKEY. Aladdin, go and get your tea now, there's a good boy.

MAGICIAN (*detaining* ALADDIN). No, the boy must stay. It concerns him chiefly.

WIDOW TWANKEY. And where do *I* come in?

MAGICIAN. You must entrust Aladdin to my care for the space of a week. We shall go on a journey from which Aladdin will return laden with wealth.

ALADDIN. D'you mean that, nunky darling?

WIDOW TWANKEY. Brother, will you swear by

this beard (*seizes his beard*) that there is no snag in it?

MAGICIAN. I will swear, darling sister, although I do not know what a snag is, or why it should be in my beard.

ALADDIN. I will go with you, Uncle, snag or no snag.

MAGICIAN. Then we will set forth immediately.

WIDOW TWANKEY. But first, dear brother, we must celebrate the occasion. (*Pushes him towards the shop.*) There's just a drop left.

MAGICIAN (*hanging back*). We must away. There is no time to lose!

ALADDIN. I'm ready when you are, Uncle.

WIDOW TWANKEY. Well, he's not ready yet. Nunky's going to have a little drop of something to warm him up for the journey.

(*She hustles him into the shop. Music for finale.* CHORUS *enter for final chorus, with* ALADDIN *as central figure.* WIDOW TWANKEY *and* MAGICIAN *reappear while music continues,* WIDOW TWANKEY *carrying* ALADDIN'S *bundle. Business of saying good-bye.* MAGICIAN *takes* ALADDIN'S *arm and leads him up stage.* CHORUS *register farewell,* WIDOW TWANKEY *blowing kisses.*)

CURTAIN.

ACT II

Scene 1.

Outside the Cave.

(*Drop scene. Backcloth representing rocks.*)

(*Enter* Magician *and* Aladdin r.)

ALADDIN. Have we much farther to go, Uncle?
MAGICIAN (*poking about with his staff*). This is the spot. The gold is hereabouts.
ALADDIN. I've got the creeps, Uncle.
MAGICIAN. The creeps? What are they, boy? I know not the word.
ALADDIN. I've got the wind up, Uncle.
MAGICIAN. How can that be? There is no wind here. All is calm and peaceful.

(*Groans and mutterings off stage.*)

ALADDIN. What's that?
MAGICIAN. Only the evil spirits of the cave. (*Aside.*) They cannot harm us while I have the ring.
ALADDIN. I don't like the look of things. I can't see.
MAGICIAN. Have patience, boy, and you will see much that you like the look of. Gold and precious stones! Now for the great experiment!

(Magician *rubs his finger vigorously.*)

ALADDIN. Have you got chilblains, Uncle?
MAGICIAN (*agitated*). When I rub the ring, the slave should appear. Can you see the slave or am I going blind?
ALADDIN. I think *I* must be going blind, Uncle, because I can't see the ring.

MAGICIAN (*staring stupidly at his hand*). It's gone! I must have dropped it.

(*They peer about on the ground.*)

ALADDIN. You're *sure* you had it when you started?

MAGICIAN (*irritably*). I *never* go out without it.

ALADDIN. Did you take it off when you had your bath this morning?

MAGICIAN. I didn't have a bath this morning.

ALADDIN. Have you looked in your waistcoat pocket?

MAGICIAN (*angrily*). I don't wear waistcoats.

ALADDIN. I say, nunky, wouldn't you look funny in a waistcoat? (*Laughs.*)

MAGICIAN (*in a rage*). The ring! The ring! Look for the ring!

(*They renew their search.*)

ALADDIN. Uncle, when you grow up and want to get married, you'll look an awful ass if you can't find the ring.

(*They collide with their heads together.* MAGICIAN *roars with pain.* ALADDIN *sits down, rubbing his head.*)

Uncle, I can see rings now.

MAGICIAN (*bending over him excitedly*). Where? Where?

ALADDIN (*stabbing the air in front of him with his finger*). There! One, two, three! Diamond rings! Oh, they've gone now.

(ALADDIN *leans over and fixes his eyes on the* MAGICIAN's *shoe. Catches hold of it suddenly.* MAGICIAN *struggles.*)

Steady, Uncle. Keep quiet a moment. It won't hurt. (*Draws the ring out of the* MAGICIAN's *shoe.*) That's a funny place to carry your spare wheel.

MAGICIAN (*snatching the ring*). Ah! We are saved.

ALADDIN. Now you can do your little trick, can't you?

(MAGICIAN *rubs ring. Flash.* SLAVE OF THE RING *appears* L.)

SLAVE OF THE RING. I am the Slave of the Ring. What are your commands?

ALADDIN. Uncle, introduce me, please.

MAGICIAN. Stand back, boy. You are but mortal and cannot touch her.

ALADDIN. I should like to give her a kiss.

SLAVE OF THE RING (*dancing round*). I am not for such as you. I am a disembodied spirit. What are your commands, please? Hurry up. I fade very quickly in the light.

ALADDIN. I command you to have this waltz with me.

SLAVE OF THE RING (*laughing*). I do not dance with mortals.

MAGICIAN. She obeys only the master of the ring. Slave, I have but one request. Reveal to me the entrance to the cave of treasure.

SLAVE OF THE RING. That is an easy task; but you must take the consequences, Master, for beyond the threshold of the cave my power ceases. Behold!

(*She waves her wand. Flash and explosion. The rock slides back, revealing the entrance to the cave* L.C. *and the* SLAVE OF THE RING *disappears into cave.*)

ALADDIN. Where's she gone, Uncle? Through that hole? I'll pop in and see.

MAGICIAN (*stopping him*). Have a care, you little fool. The cave is bewitched. Do exactly as I tell you and nothing more. Enter the cave and touch nothing that you see, save only an ancient lamp that lies upon a shelf. Bring the lamp to me here with all dispatch.

ALADDIN. If that's all you want, Uncle, you can fetch it yourself.

MAGICIAN. My old eyes are dim with age, Aladdin. I should not see the lamp. Your eyes are sharp. You can take this ring. It will protect you. (*Turns away and pulls off ring.*)

ALADDIN (*aside*). Now, I wonder what the old bird wants with that lamp. I'll have a good look at it before I give it up.

MAGICIAN. Here, boy. (*Gives ring.*) Wear it on your finger.

ALADDIN (*taking the ring*). So long, nunky. Expect me when you see me.

(ALADDIN *vanishes into the cave.*)

MAGICIAN (*rubbing his hands with glee*). Ha, ha! The lamp's as good as mine. World power at last! None will know whence comes my power or the wealth that grows around me in a single night. There's the boy to be reckoned with, though. What if he should guess the secret? I must think of a plan to silence that cackling tongue of his. (*Crosses* R. *and turns his back on the entrance.*)

ALADDIN (*poking his head round the side*). So that's his little game! Two can play at that, old whiskerface. I'll lead you a dance before I've done with you.

(ALADDIN *disappears.*)

MAGICIAN (*turns towards entrance and listens. Calls out*). Aladdin! Are you there?

ALADDIN (*off stage*). Yes, Uncle darling.

MAGICIAN. Have you got the lamp?

ALADDIN. Have I got the *what*, Uncle darling?

MAGICIAN (*getting excited*). The lamp, boy! The lamp!

ALADDIN. How d'you spell it, Uncle?

MAGICIAN (*groaning and clutching at his beard*)! This rascal boy will drive me mad.

ALADDIN. If you mean the lamp, Uncle, I've got that.

MAGICIAN (*eagerly*). Give it to me! Give it to me!

ALADDIN. Here it is. Kneel down.

(MAGICIAN *kneels down at the entrance.*)

Lean forward, Uncle.

(MAGICIAN *puts his head through the entrance.* ALADDIN *claps a wicker basket over his head.* MAGICIAN *staggers about, trying to get the basket off. He flings it away and goes into a towering rage.*)

ALADDIN AND THE WONDERFUL LAMP. 23

MAGICIAN. Is this what you call the lamp?
ALADDIN. No, Uncle. *I've* got the lamp. *You've* got the lamp-shade. Ha, ha, ha!
MAGICIAN. You shall die for this, you crazy loon. Give me the lamp or I'll be revenged upon you for your schoolboy tricks.
ALADDIN. Not likely, old twister. I found it first.
MAGICIAN. Enough! You've sealed your doom. Now you shall die a long and lingering death within the cave. What-ho! There, slave! Close the rock!

(MAGICIAN *makes a pass. Explosion and* BLACK OUT. *During the black out, the drop is lifted for*

SCENE 2.

Inside the Cave, with side entrances.)

(ALADDIN *is discovered, trying to get out of the cave.*)

ALADDIN. Uncle! Uncle! I'll give you the lamp. I'll give you the lamp, Uncle. Do you hear me? (*He listens.*) No answer! He's shut me in and he's gone away. What did I call him uncle for? He's not my uncle! He's a fiend to shut a poor boy up in a cave like this. Is there no other way out? (*He runs round, looking for an exit.*)

(*Sounds of mocking laughter off stage.*)

What's that? (*He listens again.*) I'm not frightened. Not a bit. (*His knees begin to shake.*) I *won't* be frightened. (*Knees shake harder.*) I rather *like* being here, really. (*More shaking.*) I wouldn't have missed it for *anything*.

(*Mocking laughter again.*)

(*He gets a sudden fright and calls out.*) "Help! Help!" No, that's no good. There—there's nobody at home. What *shall* I do? (*Thinks and has a brain-wave.*) I know. Of course! The ring! Old whiskerface worked the miracle. Why shouldn't I have a try? Here goes.

(*Rubs ring. Flash.* SLAVE OF THE RING *appears* R.)

SLAVE OF THE RING. I am the Slave of the Ring. What are your commands?

ALADDIN. Thank goodness. If you hadn't turned up, I don't know what I should have done.

SLAVE OF THE RING. I never fail to answer the ring.

ALADDIN. I say, why did you run away from me just now?

SLAVE OF THE RING (*dancing round*). I had received my orders from one who owns the ring. Now you have the ring, I am *your* slave.

ALADDIN. To do what I like with?

SLAVE OF THE RING. Oh, no. Only to obey your orders.

ALADDIN. What a pity. You are so beautiful I should like to take you home.

SLAVE OF THE RING. What would be the use of that? You would not see me, unless you rubbed the ring.

ALADDIN. Suppose I kept on rubbing the ring all day long. You'd have to appear every time, wouldn't you?

SLAVE OF THE RING. You must only send for me when you are in urgent need. What is your trouble now?

ALADDIN. I can't get out.

SLAVE OF THE RING. I have no power in this cave. It belongs to the Slave of the Lamp.

ALADDIN. Please tell me how to summon him.

SLAVE OF THE RING. That I cannot do. You must find out for yourself.

(SLAVE OF THE RING *turns to go.*)

ALADDIN. You're not going, are you?

SLAVE OF THE RING. It is written that the Slave of the Ring and the Slave of the Lamp must not meet over the same client. Professional etiquette, you know.

(SLAVE OF THE RING *disappears* R.)

ALADDIN. So *that's* why old whiskerface wanted the lamp so badly! What a good thing I didn't give it to him.

(*Takes lamp down from shelf.*)

It doesn't look as if it was worth much. Perhaps there's something written on it. I'll just rub some of the dirt off.

(*Rubs lamp. Flash.* SLAVE OF THE LAMP *appears* L.)

SLAVE OF THE LAMP. I am the Slave of the Lamp and am ready to obey your commands.

ALADDIN. Are—are you the landlord?

SLAVE OF THE LAMP. I am not here to answer questions. You must give me an order. You must say always: "I command you."

ALADDIN. I command you——

SLAVE OF THE LAMP. That's better.

ALADDIN. I command you to get me out of this dreadful cave.

SLAVE OF THE LAMP. That is easy. Where do you wish to go?

ALADDIN. I want to go home.

(SLAVE OF THE LAMP *walks* L. *and makes a pass over the ground.*)

SLAVE OF THE LAMP. Stand on this spot.

(ALADDIN *walks towards exit* L.)

Shut your eyes. Now—JUMP!

BLACK OUT.

(*Lights up.* ALADDIN *has disappeared.* SLAVE OF THE LAMP *performs a wild dance round the stage.* SLAVE OF THE RING *enters. They perform a characteristic dance together.* FAIRIES *enter and the dance develops into a Fairy Ballet for Finale.*)

Scene 3.

Widow Twankey's *Home* (*Interior*).

(*Large table down* L., *plenty of chairs. Entrance through doors up* R. *and up* L.)

(*Opens with dance of Chinese girls.* Widow Twankey *enters with broom and sweeps them off. Plenty of dust.*)

Widow Twankey. Now, come on,—outside, all of you. This isn't a "Pally de donce." (*Trips over broom and falls. Laughter from girls.*)

Girls. And it isn't an ice-rink.

Widow Twankey. What did you say?

Girls. We said it wasn't an ice-rink.

Widow Twankey. Oh, I thought you were making an accusation. Not that I couldn't do with a "nice drink" just now. I'm that flurried. (*Getting up.*) Now, be off with you all. Can't you see I'm busy?

(*She raises more dust. Girls go off, coughing.* Sing-Sing *comes in through door* R., *singing his song as in Act I, gets into the dust and sneezes violently.*)

Sing-Sing. Ah, Mrs. Twankey. (*Sneeze.*) Having a clean up?

Widow Twankey. No, I'm having a brush down.

Sing-Sing. There's a touch of spring in the air. (*Sneeze.*)

Widow Twankey. Of course, you *would* say that, seeing as it's Christmas-time.

Sing-Sing. Seeing you, Mrs. Twankey, always makes me feel springlike. In the spring a young man's fancy lightly turns to thoughts of—— (*Loud sneezing.*)

Widow Twankey. Now, Mr. Sing, d'you mind taking your hay-fever somewhere else? I'm very busy getting ready for the party.

Sing-Sing. Party, Mrs. Twankey? Has Aladdin come back?

Widow Twankey (*still sweeping*). Yes, he's come back, the young scamp.

ALADDIN AND THE WONDERFUL LAMP. 27

SING-SING. What about the uncle?

WIDOW TWANKEY. Ah! That's what *I* want to know. That old man has bats in his belfry, Mr. Sing. He took our Aladdin away and shut him in a cave. I knew there was a snag somewhere.

SING-SING. But how did Aladdin get out?

WIDOW TWANKEY. You'd better ask him. He's pitched me a yarn that makes me think he's gone off his chump, too. He's going about the place singing and shouting that he's made his fortune.

SING-SING. Ha, ha! He's found the treasure.

WIDOW TWANKEY. He's found a darned old lamp, that's all, as far as I can make out. Anyone would think he'd got the Rajah's Ruby. Now he wants me to give a tea-party. There's nothing in the house, but that don't seem to worry him. However, I suppose I've got to be the fond mother and humour the young rascal.

(ALADDIN *runs in through door* L.)

ALADDIN. Cheer up, Mother. Our troubles are all over. Look!

(*Holds up the lamp.*)

WIDOW TWANKEY. There you are, Mr. Sing. That's what he's brought. I don't know whether you can make anything out of it. I can't.

SING-SING (*looking at lamp very closely*). Looks to me like a lamp.

ALADDIN. It *is* a lamp. (*Laughs.*)

SING-SING. It is certainly a very curious old lamp. Is there anything written on it?

(*He is about to rub the lamp.* ALADDIN *stops him.*)

ALADDIN. Don't do that, Mr. Sing. You'll get a nasty shock. (*Takes lamp away.*)

SING-SING. Is it—is it electrified?

ALADDIN. No. (*Mysteriously.*) It's bewitched!

WIDOW TWANKEY. It's be-whatted?

ALADDIN. No, bewitched. Can you stand a shock, Mother?

WIDOW TWANKEY. Go on. I'll buy it.
ALADDIN. Then, watch this!

(ALADDIN *rubs lamp. Flash in doorway* L. SLAVE OF THE LAMP *appears.* WIDOW TWANKEY *and* SING-SING *fall over backwards, sit up and look round stupidly.*)

SLAVE OF THE LAMP. What are your commands?
ALADDIN. Ask for anything you like, Mother, and you'll get it.
WIDOW TWANKEY (*rubbing head*). I've *got* something, thank you; and I didn't ask for it, either. Did you knock me down, Mr. Sing?
SING-SING (*rubbing his head*). I was going to ask *you* that question, Mrs. Twankey.
WIDOW TWANKEY. I could do with a good stiff brandy, after that.
ALADDIN. Let refreshments be brought.

(SLAVE OF THE LAMP *bows and disappears through the doorway* L. *Immediately two attendants appear, bearing an enormous bottle and three drinking cups.*)

WIDOW TWANKEY. Well, that's pretty nippy!
SING-SING. Most remarkable!

(*One attendant is pouring out from the bottle.*)

WIDOW TWANKEY (*pretending not to notice*). Do we have to say "When"?
ALADDIN. No. Have as much as you like.
WIDOW TWANKEY. You know, there's a *snag* in this somewhere.

(*The cups are handed round.*)

(*Taking hers.*) Thank you, my man. (*They all drink.*) It's the real stuff!
SING-SING (*spluttering*). No doubt about it.
WIDOW TWANKEY. Have another?
SING-SING. To keep *you* company, Mrs. Twankey.

(*The cups are filled and emptied again.*)

I'd like to know how it's done.

ALADDIN AND THE WONDERFUL LAMP.

WIDOW TWANKEY. I'm not worrying, Mr. Sing. I just take things as they come. (*Holds out her cup for more.*)

ALADDIN. Mustn't have too much, Mother. I want you to be the right side up for the party. We're going to make a splash.

WIDOW TWANKEY (*still holding out cup and pretending not to hear very well*). No splash, thank you. I always think soda weakens the taste.

(ALADDIN *claps his hand and the attendants walk off with the bottle, followed by* ALADDIN.)

I *knew* there was a snag in it somewhere.

(*Violent knocking off stage.*)

There they are! Now, Mr. Sing, you can stand at my right hand and receive the guests with me.

SING-SING. Do I have to kiss them?

WIDOW TWANKEY. Not unless they kiss you first —which isn't likely. Just shake hands and say: "Quite well, thank you." That's all. The successful hostess always agrees with everybody. It promotes harmony. Especially at tea-parties like this one, where there isn't anything to eat. You watch me.

(*The guests arrive in couples* (R.) *and pass down to table* L.C.)

FIRST GUEST. So good of you to ask us to tea, Mrs. Twankey.

WIDOW TWANKEY (*shaking hands*). Of *course* it was.

SECOND GUEST. Here we are, Mrs. Twankey.

WIDOW TWANKEY (*shaking hands*). Of *course* you are.

THIRD GUEST. Ah, Mrs. Twankey, you seem to get younger every day.

WIDOW TWANKEY. Yes, I know.

FOURTH GUEST. So sorry we're late.

WIDOW TWANKEY. Not at all. It's a pleasure.

(*The "welcoming" business goes on until all the guests have arrived.* ALADDIN *comes in last, pretending to be a guest.*)

ALADDIN. Ah, Mrs. Twankey. I haven't seen you for *years*.

(WIDOW TWANKEY, *who is about to "agree," sees who it is and gives him a cuff over the head.*)

WIDOW TWANKEY. That boy will be the death of me, with his pranks.

(SING-SING *says* " Quite well, thank you " *monotonously to each couple as they pass in and offers his hand. Nobody takes any notice of him and he gets more and more depressed until, as the last couple come in, he is on the verge of tears and retires up stage, crestfallen.*)

ALADDIN (*coming down* C.). What about some tea, Mother?

WIDOW TWANKEY. You may well ask " What about it ! " I've told you before, there's nothing——

(ALADDIN *puts his hand over her mouth.*)

ALADDIN. Nothing to stop us having it now. Let us ring for tea.

(ALADDIN *rubs lamp. A flash in doorway* L. SLAVE OF THE LAMP *appears* L.)

Let tea be served at once.

SLAVE OF THE LAMP (*bowing*). Your commands shall be obeyed. (*Exits.*)

FIRST GUEST. Is that your new maid, Mrs. Twankey?

WIDOW TWANKEY (*rising to the occasion*). Er—— Yes, that's my new maid. That's right.

SECOND GUEST. Where *did* you get her?

WIDOW TWANKEY. Oh, from the Servants' Agency, you know.

SECOND GUEST. Did you say " *Servants'* Agency " or " *Circus* Agency " ?

(*Attendants enter* L. *with tray, laden with refreshments, which they place on the table. Everybody registers amazement.*)

THIRD GUEST. I *do* call that smart work.

ALADDIN. Our new maid can do anything, can't she, Mother?

WIDOW TWANKEY. Yes, my boy, if you say so. I'm afraid I haven't got used to her yet.

ALADDIN (*pushing* SING-SING *forward*). Now then, Mr. Sing, help yourself. Don't look as if you'd seen a ghost.

SING-SING (*trembling*). I think I *have* seen a ghost, Master Aladdin.

ALADDIN. You'll be all right when you've had something to eat.

SING-SING (*pointing to the table*). Is it—is it all *paid* for?

ALADDIN. Don't ask questions. Take what the rich man gives you and be thankful.

SECOND GUEST. We didn't know you'd come into money, Aladdin. How *did* you do it?

ALADDIN. That's a secret known only to mother and me.

WIDOW TWANKEY (*rising, cup in hand*). Here's luck to Aladdin and his Wonderful——

(ALADDIN *puts his hand over her mouth again.*)

—and his wonderful mother.

THIRD GUEST. *I* know. You've gone into the film business.

ALADDIN. Now, my friends, just keep a tight hold on yourselves, or what I'm going to tell you will make you jump out of your skins. I'm going to be the biggest showman this country's ever seen, and my Nineteen-thirty Peking Revue is going to shake the world, because it's all going to be *Real.* If I'm not very much mistaken, my friends, you'll be proud to know me shortly. I'm going in for Magic.

(*Laughter from guests.*)

I'm going to build a palace that will make the Emperor's look like the village bungalow. And to finish everything off nicely, I'm going to marry the Emperor's daughter.

(*More laughter.*)

SECOND GUEST. You know, your son ought to be put away, Mrs. Twankey.

(WIDOW TWANKEY *dances round the stage, looking very knowing.*)

WIDOW TWANKEY. You don't know these things! All we've got to do is to rub the——

(*Business of* ALADDIN *shutting her up again.*)

—rub the Emperor up the right way and there you are!

SING-SING. It's all very well to say "There you are," but *where* are we? I think we must all be dreaming.

ALADDIN. And *you're* having a nightmare by the look of your face.

SING-SING. I don't know whether I'm on my head or my heels.

FIRST GUEST. *I* think we ought to be going. I don't like the look of this. It's my belief the Twankeys are wonky.

WIDOW TWANKEY (*shouting*). The Twankeys *wonky!* What d'you mean? You can't insult a Twankey more than once, young woman!

SECOND GUEST. *I* think there's something fishy about it.

WIDOW TWANKEY. Fishy! There's nothing "fishy" about a tea-party, unless the guests come from Billingsgate!

THIRD GUEST (*rising*). Let's go. We don't want to be mixed up with a black-hand gang.

(*Guests rise and make for the door* R.)

WIDOW TWANKEY (*to* ALADDIN, *who is shaking with laughter*). Aladdin, is that all you can do? Stand there and laugh when your mother is being insulted?

(*The couples go off, each with a cutting remark at* WIDOW TWANKEY, *who is fuming with anger.*)

FIRST GUEST. Good-bye, Mrs. Twankey. Give my kind regards to the Emperor, won't you? (*Exit laughing.*)

SECOND GUEST. *And* to the Emperor's daughter. (*Exit laughing.*)

THIRD GUEST. When you're put away, you can say you're the Queen of Sheba. Nobody will contradict you then.

(*Etc., etc.*)

WIDOW TWANKEY (*looking round for someone to vent her wrath upon*). Well, Mr. Sing, are you going to join in the chorus and exit laughing?

SING-SING. Mrs. Twankey, I'll stick to you through thick and thin. (*Kisses his hand to her.*)

WIDOW TWANKEY. *Stick* to me! What d'you think I am—a flypaper? This is a fine state of affairs for a Twankey, I'm sure. First I'm called "Wonky," then I'm told I've got black hands, and there's my son, who ought to be the prop of his mother at a time like this, laughing like a hyena.

ALADDIN. What does it matter what the neighbours say, Mother? When I've married the Princess, you can snap your fingers at everybody. Now I'm going to rub the lamp and summon the Princess. She'll have to come—you see.

WIDOW TWANKEY. Oh, Aladdin—you and your magic lantern will be the death of me.

(ALADDIN *rubs lamp.* SLAVE OF THE LAMP *appears as before.*)

SLAVE OF THE LAMP. What are your commands, Master?

ALADDIN. Let Princess Baldroubadour be brought here immediately.

(SLAVE OF THE LAMP *bows and retires.*)

C

WIDOW TWANKEY. She seems to take it very calmly.
SING-SING. Just as if you'd sent her out to buy half a pound of rice.
ALADDIN. Listen!
WIDOW TWANKEY. What is it?
ALADDIN. Nothing!
SING-SING. Yes, that's what I heard!

(*Loud rattle off stage.*)

Here she comes.
WIDOW TWANKEY. That's the nine-o'clock bus, stupid. She wouldn't be on that.
ALADDIN. Perhaps she'll come on a magic carpet.
WIDOW TWANKEY. Not through *our* front door!
ALADDIN. She ought to be here by now. Something's gone wrong.
WIDOW TWANKEY. Press button B and get your money back.
SING-SING (*suddenly*). I say!
ALADDIN. } What?
WIDOW TWANKEY. }
SING-SING. Supposing the Princess is in her bath?
ALADDIN. She'll have to come—wherever she is!
SING-SING. Will she come without any——
WIDOW TWANKEY. Difficulty? Let's hope so.
ALADDIN. I never thought of that. I can't propose to the Princess if she hasn't got any——
WIDOW TWANKEY. Common sense. Of course you can't.
ALADDIN. What an awful thought! If she arrives in a state of——
WIDOW TWANKEY. Uncertainty, things will be very awkward. I, as a respectable widow, shall make a dignified exit before it's too late. Come, Mr. Sing——
SING-SING. I—I think I shall stay and see the fun.
WIDOW TWANKEY (*sternly*). Mr. Sing, did you not promise to *stick* to me?
SING-SING. You repulsed me, Mrs. Twankey, with a reference to flypapers.

ALADDIN AND THE WONDERFUL LAMP. 35

WIDOW TWANKEY. On this occasion—as you so much resemble an insect—you *shall* stick to me.
(*Drags him off with her* R.)

ALADDIN. Perhaps it's just as well they didn't stay. A chaperone for the Princess would be rather—early Victorian. But why doesn't she come? Can anything have happened? Perhaps she *is* here—invisible—waiting for me to call her.

(*Goes on his knees and calls* "Princess, Princess."

BALDROUBADOUR *appears in the doorway* L., *her face covered by a veil.*)

BALDROUBADOUR. Who calls?

ALADDIN. It is I—Aladdin—your lover.

BALDROUBADOUR. The voice is strangely like the voice of my dreams.

ALADDIN. But now you are awake, Princess. Your dreams perhaps are coming true.

BALDROUBADOUR. What magic power is this, that now surrounds me! I have been lifted from my boudoir without warning and hurled through space. I am feeling a little—air-sick, I think.

ALADDIN. I'm afraid I am to blame, Princess. But my love for you is so strong that I can stop at nothing to gain your hand.

BALDROUBADOUR. You are a Man of Mystery, Aladdin.

ALADDIN. Yes, Princess.

BALDROUBADOUR (*sighing deeply*). I love—mysterious men.

ALADDIN (*approaching her as if to lift her veil*). May I—may I—draw the blind?

BALDROUBADOUR. I beg your pardon!

ALADDIN. May I—proceed with the Unveiling Ceremony?

BALDROUBADOUR. No man has ever dared to lift my veil.

ALADDIN. Until Aladdin came and put them all to shame.

(*Lifts her veil with a sudden movement.*)

BALDROUBADOUR. For this uncalled-for behaviour, you shall be severely——
ALADDIN. Punished?
BALDROUBADOUR. Rewarded.

(*She leans over and kisses him.* WIDOW TWANKEY, *appearing in doorway* R., *coughs loudly.* SING-SING *is behind her, and follows her in.*)

ALADDIN (*embarrassed*). Mother—er—this is, this is——

WIDOW TWANKEY (*coming forward and grasping* BALDROUBADOUR'S *hand*). This is a pleasant surprise. Please to meet you, my dear. Aladdin said you might drop in one of these days. I'm his dear mamma——

(SING-SING *has fallen on his knees and is prostrating himself before* BALDROUBADOUR.)

—and the gentleman doing the breathing exercises, over there, is Mr. Sing-Sing. Now we all know each other. Will you take a little something?

BALDROUBADOUR. Yes, thank you. I'm going to take——

WIDOW TWANKEY. A glass of sherry?

BALDROUBADOUR. No. A husband. Aladdin.

WIDOW TWANKEY. My son—to marry the Princess!

BALDROUBADOUR. I love him. He's so strong and so—mysterious.

WIDOW TWANKEY (*looking round carefully*). Catch me, Mr. Sing. I think I'm going to faint. (*She falls on to* SING-SING, *who drags her off* R.)

(*Music for finale. Chorus enters* L. *and* R. CURTAIN *can be brought down either on a duet for* ALADDIN *and* BALDROUBADOUR, *assisted by chorus, or by full chorus number.*)

ACT III

SCENE I

Aladdin's Palace.

Side entrances and entrance back C., *down steps. Couch down* R.

(*Opening Chorus of Chinese Courtiers.*)

(*Enter* MUSTAPHA, *the Grand Vizier, back* C.)

MUSTAPHA. Ladies and Gentlemen of the Court, you are hereby ordered to salute in the customary manner His Imperial and Celestial Highness, the Emperor of China.

(*Chorus bend low, with their foreheads to the ground, dressing the stage for entrance of* EMPEROR. *Music.* EMPEROR *comes on back* C.)

EMPEROR. Behold, your Emperor!

(*Chorus remain prostrate.*)

(*Annoyed.*) What's the use of my saying " Behold " if they don't " behold " ?

(*Chorus rise and shout* " Hail! O Emperor! " *and make their exits* R. *and* L. *during* EMPEROR'S *speech.*)

That's better. I like a *little* notice taken of me. (*To* MUSTAPHA.) And why is my son-in-law not here? Did I not give orders for Prince Aladdin to receive me in person, when I pay him a state visit?

MUSTAPHA. Prince Aladdin is in his bath, your Majesty, and will be down shortly.

EMPEROR. Observe, good Mustapha, his colossal impudence. He keeps me waiting! I am beginning to

38 ALADDIN AND THE WONDERFUL LAMP.

wonder who *is* now the Emperor of China. I gave him my daughter—but not the throne of China.

MUSTAPHA. Your Majesty must not forget that financially——

EMPEROR. Yes. Quite. That's the devil of it. He's so confoundedly **rich**. A word in your ear, good Mustapha.

(*He leads* MUSTAPHA *down stage mysteriously.*)

Have you succeeded in discovering the source of Aladdin's wealth?

MUSTAPHA. Not yet, O Emperor, but I am on the track. Has your Majesty heard of Professor Ho Hi Ho?

EMPEROR. Ho Hi who?

MUSTAPHA. No. Ho Hi Ho.

EMPEROR. Ho Hi see.

MUSTAPHA. He claims to have magic powers and craves an audience.

EMPEROR. What does he do?

MUSTAPHA. Craves an audience.

EMPEROR. You mean, he wants to see me.

MUSTAPHA. Yes, O Emperor.

EMPEROR. Then, why don't you say so? Send for him at once.

(*Exit* MUSTAPHA R., *bowing.*)

Much as I hate professors, especially magic ones, I must grasp every opportunity that presents itself. If only I knew Aladdin's secret, I would sing for joy. But as I don't—well, I'll sing for nothing.

SONG : EMPEROR.

(*Enter* MUSTAPHA *and* MAGICIAN R., *disguised as* PROFESSOR HO HI HO.)

MAGICIAN (*falling down in obeisance*). Hail, O Emperor!

EMPEROR. Rise, Professor Yo Heave Ho, and tell me your business.

MAGICIAN (*fingering his beard*). I am engaged in research work, O Emperor.

EMPEROR. You mean, you're looking for something?
MAGICIAN. Yes, Emperor. (*Fingers beard.*)
EMPEROR. Then why don't you say so? Do you expect to find it in your beard?
MAGICIAN. I am a stranger and unknown in this city. It is necessary for the exercise of my powers that I have a free pass into the principal buildings of Peking.
EMPEROR. Including this palace?
MAGICIAN (*looking round him anxiously*). Including this palace.
EMPEROR. Humph! (*Takes* MUSTAPHA *on one side while* MAGICIAN *continues to look round him anxiously as if seeking something.*) A queer bird, this professor. What do you think of him?
MUSTAPHA. I have put him through several tests, your Majesty. A genuine magician. Performed several tricks in front of my very eyes and I couldn't see how they were done.
EMPEROR. Such as——?
MUSTAPHA. Well, your Majesty, he produced an Austin Seven from his left pocket, swallowed it and brought it out of his right ear.
EMPEROR. Marvellous. (*Turns to* MAGICIAN.) We will grant you, Professor, the Freedom of the City. In return for this favour, you shall perform tricks twice nightly before the Chinese Court.
MAGICIAN (*rubbing his hands with satisfaction*). If your Majesty will give me time, I will perform a feat that will astonish not only China, but the whole world.

(*Exit* MAGICIAN R.)

(*Cheers off stage for* ALADDIN'S *entrance.*)

MUSTAPHA. The Prince is approaching, your Majesty.
EMPEROR (*listening*). Do they always cheer him like that?
MUSTAPHA. Aladdin is very popular.
EMPEROR. More popular than I?
MUSTAPHA. Aladdin is very rich.
EMPEROR. Humph! (*Feels his nose.*) Good Mus-

tapha, you have the royal permission to look me in the face.

MUSTAPHA (*doing so*). It is an unexpected honour, your Majesty.

EMPEROR. Do you observe anything wrong with my nose?

MUSTAPHA. Nothing at all, your Majesty.

EMPEROR (*turning away*). It feels out of joint!

(*Music.*)

(*Enter* ALADDIN *back* C.)

ALADDIN. Good morning, father-in-law. Good morning, Grand Vizier. I trust you both have that Kruschen feeling.

EMPEROR. That is our business. It is *your* business to be here when I arrive. After all, I *am* the Emperor of China.

ALADDIN. Sorry, Governor. You see, I don't know the ropes. I wasn't brought up at Court. I was caught and brought up. Oh, I say, that's rather a good one. (*Laughs.*)

MUSTAPHA (*coughing nervously*). His Majesty does not permit jokes to be made before lunch.

ALADDIN. Quite. I had forgotten the Royal Liver. (*Slaps the* EMPEROR *on the back.*) Well, Aged Parent, what do you think of your daughter's new home? Are you satisfied?

EMPEROR. It puts the Royal Palace in the shade, and, therefore, it is in very bad taste.

ALADDIN. Say the word, Pa, and you shall have as fine a palace as this, and finer.

EMPEROR (*gloating*). Ah! Then I *will* say the word. It must be fitted with every modern convenience.

ALADDIN. You have only to name them, sir.

EMPEROR. Now, let me see—just jot them down, Mustapha.

(MUSTAPHA *takes out large notebook and pencil and makes notes.*)

Electric lifts to all floors, marble bathrooms, Louis

ALADDIN AND THE WONDERFUL LAMP.

Fourteenth Salon, Palm Court, American Bar, mosaic walls——

ALADDIN. And what about the roof, sir? Gold tiles or just ordinary thatch?

EMPEROR. Gold would be more distinctive.

ALADDIN. Very good, sir. And when did you wish to move in?

EMPEROR. To-morrow morning.

ALADDIN. It shall be ready for you down to the smallest detail.

MUSTAPHA. Amazing! Our workmen could not do it in less than twelve months, your Majesty.

ALADDIN. If you will choose a site for the palace, sir, operations will commence at nightfall.

EMPEROR. At nightfall?

ALADDIN. My men only work after dark.

EMPEROR. I thought there was something shady about it. Come, Mustapha, let us go and choose a site. If the trick works, we will confer upon our clever son-in-law the order of the Royal and Ancient Society of Jerry Builders.

(*Exeunt* EMPEROR *and* MUSTAPHA R.)

ALADDIN. Poor old Pa-in-law, he doesn't know how easy it is. All I've got to do is to say, "Build me a palace," and, hey presto, it's done! Talk about the romance of Big Business. It's nothing compared to Aladdin and his wonderful Luck!

SONG : ALADDIN.

(BALDROUBADOUR'S *voice heard off stage calling* "Aladdin.")

That's my sweetie! Coming for her morning kiss, bless her.

(*Enter* BALDROUBADOUR *back* C.)

Darling wife!

BALDROUBADOUR. Darling husband!

(*They embrace fervently.*)

Darling, must you leave me to-day?

ALADDIN. I am off for a day's hunting, sweet one. I shall be back at nightfall.

BALDROUBADOUR. What shall I do all day without my wonderful Aladdin?

ALADDIN. You need not be idle. You can think of me—hunting tigers in the jungle.

BALDROUBADOUR. How boring!

ALADDIN. I will bring you back a beautiful skin.

BALDROUBADOUR. I already have a beautiful skin.

(*Sound of hunting horn.*)

ALADDIN. Hark! The royal huntsmen are ready. Darling, I must love you and leave you.

(*Noise of barking.*)

My pack of Pekingese are impatient to be off. Hear how they give tongue.

BALDROUBADOUR. Aladdin, promise me you'll take care of yourself. I am uneasy when you are away.

ALADDIN. Take this ring, dearest. (*Gives ring.*) It will protect you. If you need help while I'm away, rub the ring.

(ALADDIN *kisses her and runs off back* C. BALDROUBADOUR *waves her hand in farewell and comes down* C.)

BALDROUBADOUR. "If you need help, rub the ring." What good can that do? "Pop the ring" would be a more practical suggestion. I hope I shan't have to do either.

(*Arranges herself on couch* R. *and claps her hands.*)

(*Enter* ESMERALDA L., *bowing.*)

ESMERALDA. What is your gracious will, Princess?

BALDROUBADOUR. I am bored, Esmeralda, and would be amused. Summon the dancers.

(*Exit* ESMERALDA R., *bowing.*)

(*Opportunity here for special dance number.*)

(ESMERALDA *returns.*)

I am in need of still further amusement, Esmeralda. Tell me a funny story.

ESMERALDA (*sitting down beside the couch and beginning obediently*). Once upon a time, there was a beautiful princess——

BALDROUBADOUR. No, that won't do. I shall never get a thrill from a story about a beautiful princess. It's much too near home.

ESMERALDA. I'm sorry, your Highness. (*Takes a breath and begins again.*) Once upon a time, there was a little beggar girl——

BALDROUBADOUR. No, that won't do either. I hate stories about low life.

ESMERALDA. I'm sorry, your Highness. (*Begins again.*) Once upon a time——

BALDROUBADOUR. Why must you *always* start with "once upon a time"? I always know you're going to end up with "happily ever afterwards." That kind of story is *never* funny.

(*Hubbub off stage. Shouting and sounds of jeering laughter.*)

Listen! What is that noise?

ESMERALDA. It sounds, noble Princess, as if some gentleman of the Court has just "told one."

BALDROUBADOUR. Go and tell the gentleman of the Court to come here at once.

(*Exit* ESMERALDA L.)

I will command him to tell it in the royal presence. I know that princesses are supposed not to listen to funny stories, but one must have *some* excitement when one's man is away. I hope the story won't be *too* funny. In that case, I shall have to pretend I haven't heard it.

(*More laughing and jeering off stage.* ESMERALDA *comes back, laughing.*)

ESMERALDA. There's a funny old man outside, trying to sell lamps, or something. They've been pulling his leg and he's getting so annoyed.

BALDROUBADOUR. How did he get into the palace.
ESMERALDA. Goodness knows. Here he comes.

(MAGICIAN *enters* L., *disguised as a pedlar. He is bent with age and carries a basket.*)

MAGICIAN. New lamps for old! New lamps for old! New lamps for old!

BALDROUBADOUR. He's got it wrong, hasn't he, Esmeralda? Nobody in their senses would give away a new lamp for an old one.

MAGICIAN. If the high and noble lady has an old lamp, I will give her a new one in exchange. There is no deception.

BALDROUBADOUR. Esmeralda, I am in the mood to humour this quaint old man.

ESMERALDA. I doubt if there are any old lamps in the palace, Princess.

BALDROUBADOUR. See if you can find one.

(*Exit* ESMERALDA R.)

MAGICIAN. The noble lady is most gracious and kind. I have a passion for old things.

BALDROUBADOUR. Especially for old clothes, I should imagine.

MAGICIAN. The men and women laugh at me. The children in the streets throw stones at me. They think I am trying to deceive them, the fools. But see, noble lady, what good value I give in exchange. These lamps (*holds one up*) are made of solid gold.

BALDROUBADOUR. Oh, what a sweet little lamp!

(*Enter* ESMERALDA R., *carrying* ALADDIN'S *lamp.*)

ESMERALDA. Will this do, Princess? I found it in Prince Aladdin's room. It's old enough and it's of no use.

(*As* ESMERALDA *holds out the lamp, the* MAGICIAN *makes a sudden movement and seizes her wrist. She screams and drops the lamp, which is snatched up by the* MAGICIAN.)

ALADDIN AND THE WONDERFUL LAMP.

MAGICIAN. Mine! Mine, at last!

(MAGICIAN *rubs lamp. Flash.* SLAVE OF THE LAMP *appears back* c.)

BALDROUBADOUR. What treachery is this! Call the guard!

MAGICIAN (*throwing off his disguise and laughing triumphantly*). Too late. Too late, Princess. The palace now is mine. Aladdin's doom is sealed!

(BALDROUBADOUR *collapses into* ESMERALDA'S *arms.*)

SLAVE OF THE LAMP. What are your commands, O Master?

MAGICIAN. Transport the palace as it stands to Africa.

SLAVE OF THE LAMP. It shall be done.

(SLAVE OF THE LAMP *makes a pass with her wand. Thunder is heard and lights are dimmed down.*)

ESMERALDA. Help! Help!

(*As* ESMERALDA *runs off* L., *the* MAGICIAN *rushes to the* PRINCESS *and takes her in his arms.*)

MAGICIAN. Now in my arms you'll rest content, my pretty one. Revenge is sweet!

(*The illusion of movement can be supplied by a motor-cycle engine which can be started up in the wings. In the flickering light, the* MAGICIAN *is seen carrying off* BALDROUBADOUR. *Dramatic music.*)

BLACK OUT FOR SCENE 2.

SCENE 2.

Same as Scene 1.

(WIDOW TWANKEY *is discovered creeping on* R. *in a great state of nerves.* SING-SING'S *head appears round the side of entrance back* c.)

SING-SING. Peep-bo!

(Widow Twankey *collapses with fright.* Sing-Sing *discloses himself and comes down.*)

Widow Twankey. Oh, it's you, Mr. Sing! Thank goodness you're safe. What *has* happened?

Sing-Sing. An earthquake, I should say, Mrs. Twankey. The whole palace has been rocking about.

Widow Twankey. *Rocking* about! It's been lifted up and dropped from a great height. I was about to enter the palace when it happened. I had one foot on the doorstep.

Sing-Sing. And where was the other one, Mrs. T.?

Widow Twankey. Dangling, Mr. Sing! It was left dangling in the air. Not a comfortable position for a woman of my age. I then experienced the sensation of being fired from a gun.

Sing-Sing. There is nothing shell-like about you, my love, except—if I may say so—your sweet little ears.

Widow Twankey. This is no time for compliments, however true. Have you a good bump of locality?

Sing-Sing (*rubbing his limbs*). I have several, Mrs. T. I don't know which is the best.

Widow Twankey. I mean, do you know where we are?

Sing-Sing. We're in the soup, it's clear.

Widow Twankey. *I* think it's a bit thick, but— thick or clear, there's something " soup "-ernatural about it.

(*Crash off stage.* Emperor *and* Mustapha *stagger on back* c.)

Emperor. Will somebody tell us where we are?

Widow Twankey. In the soup, your Majesty.

Mustapha. It is not possible for the Emperor to be in the soup.

Widow Twankey. Well, you can call it the Royal Consommy, if you want to be snobbish about it. It's the gravy, all the same.

ALADDIN AND THE WONDERFUL LAMP. 47

EMPEROR. Where is your flask, good Mustapha? I "must 'av" a drink.

(MUSTAPHA *brings out large flask marked "Fine Old Brandy."*)

WIDOW TWANKEY (*who is overcome by the pun*). So must I, after that. Where is *your* flask, Mr. Sing?

(SING-SING *brings out a large flask marked "Lemonade."* WIDOW TWANKEY *is about to drink when she notices the label and registers disgust.*)

Coming from *you*, Mr. Sing, the answer *would* be a lemon.

(*Throws flask back at him.*)

EMPEROR (*after drinking*). That's better. Now we must get to the bottom of this. (*Hands flask to* MUSTAPHA.)

WIDOW TWANKEY. If your Majesty will pass the bottle, I will do my best to do that.

(*Flask is handed to* WIDOW TWANKEY, *who prepares to drink. The* MAGICIAN *appears suddenly, back* C., *with folded arms, and shouts "Ha!"* WIDOW TWANKEY, *surprised over her drink, has a choking fit.*)

SING-SING. Why, it's the wicked uncle!
EMPEROR. Professor Ho Hi Ho!
MAGICIAN. Ha, ha, ha! Call me what you will, you are my prisoners. You cannot escape. You are in the heart of the African Desert.

WIDOW TWANKEY (*emptying sand out of her boot*). I thought as much.

MAGICIAN. Your Celestial Highness asked me to perform a trick. This is my trick. Is it not a good one?

(MAGICIAN *roars with laughter.*)

EMPEROR. I don't see anything funny in it—do you, Mustapha?

MUSTAPHA. The joke is in very bad taste, your Majesty. In China, it is considered bad form to kidnap the Emperor.

MAGICIAN. You shall remain in exile until my wishes are granted. What-ho, there! Bring in the Princess.

(BALDROUBADOUR *is brought on* L. *by two attendants.*)

I am smitten with the charms of the beautiful Baldroubadour and am determined to possess her. I ask you now for an answer, my sweet one.

BALDROUBADOUR (*stamping her foot*). No! No! No!

MAGICIAN. We shall see who is the stronger. I will leave you, my beauty, to the tender mercies of your affectionate father and your loving mother-in-law. If they can persuade you to be my wife, I will let them go free. If you still resist my will, I shall put them to the torture. The more you resist, the more I shall torture them.

WIDOW TWANKEY. You horrid old cave-man!

MAGICIAN. At the end of ten minutes, I shall come back for my answer.

(*Exit* MAGICIAN *back* C., *with an evil laugh.*)

BALDROUBADOUR (*on her knees*). Oh, Father, Father, what *is* going to happen? I am frightened to death of this man. What shall I do?

EMPEROR. Do, my dear daughter? Why, you'll have to be nice to him.

BALDROUBADOUR (*shrieking*). What!

EMPEROR. I don't see any other way out of it.

WIDOW TWANKEY. You must use your woman's wit, my dear. I wish *I* could have the chance to vamp him. I'd lead him a dance.

SING-SING. You can't see us tortured before your eyes.

MUSTAPHA. It is against the rules for the Emperor to suffer torture.

EMPEROR. Come, Mustapha. We will inform this bearded bandit that our daughter is ready to grant his wish. It is the only way.

WIDOW TWANKEY. Stroke his beard, my dear, and call him your "oodlums, doodlums." That will soften his heart. I know these cave-men.

(*Exeunt* EMPEROR *and* MUSTAPHA R., *followed by* WIDOW TWANKEY *and* SING-SING.)

BALDROUBADOUR. Esmeralda! Esmeralda!

(ESMERALDA *runs on* L.)

Oh, Esmeralda, I am lost! What is to be done?

ESMERALDA. Keep calm, darling Princess, and we will think out a plan. I wish I could *wring* his horrid old neck.

BALDROUBADOUR (*starting suddenly, as an idea comes to her*). *Ring*—that's it. Ring! The Ring!

ESMERALDA. What's the matter?

BALDROUBADOUR. What did Aladdin say? If you need help, rub the ring. Here it is, still on my finger. Why didn't I think of it before?

(*Rubs ring. Flash.* SLAVE OF THE RING *appears* L.)

SLAVE OF THE RING. I obey the summons, Princess, but I have no power here.

BALDROUBADOUR. Can you not help us?

SLAVE OF THE RING. Only the Slave of the Lamp can help you here. To summon her, you must regain the magic lamp.

BALDROUBADOUR. If only Aladdin were here! He would soon get it back.

SLAVE OF THE RING. Listen, O mistress. Aladdin shall be summoned to Africa. That I have the power to do. But in the meantime the magician must be overcome. Take this powder.

(SLAVE OF THE RING *gives a packet to* BALDROUBADOUR.)

It is a powerful drug and will take instant effect. Your opportunity will come when the Master of the Lamp is drinking wine. Shake the powder into his wine and he will fall into a deep sleep. The magic lamp is secured by a chain round his neck, and lies beneath his robes. Obey these instructions to the letter and your lives shall be saved.

(*Exit* SLAVE OF THE RING L.)

BALDROUBADOUR. This will require all my courage, Esmeralda. I tremble to think what will happen if that monster suspects me, beforehand.

ESMERALDA. I will stay with you, Princess, in case of need.

BALDROUBADOUR. No, you must go. He will be off his guard if he finds me alone.

ESMERALDA. I will be close at hand and will come at your call.

(*Exit* ESMERALDA L.)

(BALDROUBADOUR *hides the powder in her gown, then arranges herself among the cushions on the couch.* MAGICIAN *enters* R., *gloating over his prey.*)

MAGICIAN. Ah, my little turtle-dove, so you are going to yield to me. You are going to love me and let me kiss those rosy lips.

(*He approaches the couch.* BALDROUBADOUR *makes room for him.*)

BALDROUBADOUR. You must forgive me, sir. You would not have me be too bold at first. But be assured, I have always had a weakness for gentlemen with beards.

MAGICIAN. Ha, ha! You have changed your tune, my pretty one!

BALDROUBADOUR. You have a beautiful beard, sir.

MAGICIAN. Say you so, my chicken? Then you shall stroke it, and I will stroke your pretty cheeks. So——

(*She strokes his beard, nervously, while he caresses her.*)

You are a sensible little bird, after all. I can give you all you want. You have only to name your wish.

BALDROUBADOUR. Indeed, sir, I have but few wants, and they are simple. A little wine would please me now. Flirting always makes me so thirsty.

MAGICIAN (*claps his hands*). I am in the mood to spoil you, my beauty.

(*Attendant appears* L.)

Let wine be brought and bid the dancers prepare.

(*Exit attendant* L.)

ALADDIN AND THE WONDERFUL LAMP. 51

MAGICIAN. We will drink and be merry. The wine is the best in the land, and you will add flavour to it.

BALDROUBADOUR. I will do my best to flavour your wine, good sir.

MAGICIAN. Ha, ha! You have a saucy tongue, but that is as it should be.

(*Enter attendant* L. *with wine, which is set before them.*) Here's to Wine, Woman and Song.

(*They raise their cups.*)

Sparkling wine, beautiful woman (*he toasts her*)——

BALDROUBADOUR. And what about the song?

MAGICIAN. It is ready for my little honeycomb. (*Claps hands.*) Let the music begin.

(*An Eastern chorus number can be inserted here.*)

(*After the number, the* MAGICIAN *raises his cup to drink again.* BALDROUBADOUR *stops him with a hand on his arm.*)

BALDROUBADOUR. Hark! I thought I heard——

MAGICIAN (*putting the cup down, within her reach*). Heard what, my dove?

BALDROUBADOUR. I thought I heard Aladdin's voice.

MAGICIAN (*rising in a rage and shouting*). Aladdin!

BALDROUBADOUR. It seemed to come from over there. (*She points to entrance back* C.)

(*The* MAGICIAN *strides across and listens, with his back turned to* BALDROUBADOUR. *With a quick movement she takes the powder from its hiding-place and shakes it into his wine.*)

MAGICIAN. I hear no sound.

BALDROUBADOUR. I do not hear it now. I must have been mistaken.

MAGICIAN (*returning*). The mention of that hated name is maddening to me. His name shall never pass your lips again. I forbid it.

BALDROUBADOUR (*gaily*). Your commands shall be

obeyed. (*Raises her cup.*) Let us drink to his destruction.

MAGICIAN (*highly pleased and raising his cup*). To Aladdin's destruction.

(MAGICIAN *takes a drink from the cup.* BALDROUBADOUR *rises quickly and moves down* R.)

BALDROUBADOUR (*aside*). The deed is done. If the drug does not work, I am lost!

MAGICIAN. Not so fast, my pretty one. Would you run away from your lord and master? (*He makes a movement towards her, cup in hand, but dizziness overcomes him.*) What devil's broth is this! (*Flings cup away.*) Hold me up. I fall, I fall! (*He staggers back on to the couch, unconscious.*)

BALDROUBADOUR. And now to get the lamp.

(*As she approaches the* MAGICIAN, *he gives a loud snore, and she runs across* L., *frightened.* ALADDIN *appears, back* C.)

Aladdin! At last!

(ALADDIN *runs to her.*)

ALADDIN. Darling, here you are safe and sound!
BALDROUBADOUR (*pointing to* MAGICIAN). Look!
ALADDIN. What! Old whiskerface! Is he dead?

(*Loud snore from* MAGICIAN.)

Sounds as if he's asleep.

BALDROUBADOUR. The Lamp, Aladdin! The Lamp! He has the Lamp!

ALADDIN. But not for long. Now's our chance to strip him of his stolen goods. Stand by to catch.

(ALADDIN *searches the* MAGICIAN. *Business can be worked here, before the lamp is found, various comic articles, which can be concealed under the couch beforehand, being flung about the stage.*)

(*Finding the lamp.*) Hooray! (*Comes* C.) Now we shan't be long.

ALADDIN AND THE WONDERFUL LAMP.

(ALADDIN *rubs lamp. Flash.* SLAVE OF THE LAMP *appears* L.)

SLAVE OF THE LAMP. Master, what is your wish?

ALADDIN. Is it in your power to—wake the Sleeping Beauty? (*Points to* MAGICIAN.)

SLAVE OF THE LAMP. One touch of this wand will bring him to.

ALADDIN. Let's have a go. (*Takes wand.*) I have a word to say to this precious uncle of mine.

(ALADDIN *strikes the* MAGICIAN *with the wand.*)

Arise, Sir Whiskerface!

(MAGICIAN *wakes and staggers to his feet.*)

MAGICIAN (*holding his head*). My head! My head!

ALADDIN. If you'd been a teetotaller, Uncle, this wouldn't have happened. Now you've lost the lamp and you're lucky not to have lost your head as well.

MAGICIAN (*taking in the situation*). Betrayed!—By a woman!

ALADDIN. The usual fate of men who think they are clever.

MAGICIAN. You have not finished with me yet. I have other methods. We shall meet again.

ALADDIN. But not this year. The season's over.

(ALADDIN *pulls a long nose at the* MAGICIAN, *who goes off in a rage* R.)

(*To* SLAVE OF THE LAMP.) Now, James, we're ready when you are.

SLAVE OF THE LAMP. Your commands, O Master?

ALADDIN. Home, James—and no stopping on the way.

SLAVE OF THE LAMP. That's easily done.

(SLAVE OF THE LAMP *waves her wand. Noise and lighting effects as before. The* EMPEROR, MUSTAPHA, WIDOW TWANKEY *and* SING-SING *enter,* L. *and* R., *turning round and round and bumping into each other. Comic effects for the flying palace can be obtained by moving the scenery itself. This business ad lib. until a whistle is blown.*)

ALADDIN. All change for Peking.

(*Orchestra strikes up a march tune. Chorus enter from both wings, march round and form up* L. *and* R., *principals in the* C.)

SING-SING. Here's to China, Home and Beauty—and especially Beauty. (*Kisses* WIDOW TWANKEY.)

WIDOW TWANKEY (*singing*). There's no place like home!

BALDROUBADOUR. This is the happiest moment of my life.

WIDOW TWANKEY (*dancing round*). She's twenty-one to-day. She's twenty-one to-day.

MUSTAPHA. Silence for the Emperor of China!

EMPEROR. I am getting on in years, and in my old age I would be free from the cares of state. I could not place them in better hands than those of my clever son-in-law. I abdicate, in favour of Prince Aladdin.

ALADDIN. A great and noble gesture, your Majesty. I accept your offer.

WIDOW TWANKEY. And I, dear Mr. Sing, accept yours. (*Falling into* SING-SING'S *arms.*)

EMPEROR. Approach, dear daughter, and salute your royal husband. (*He leads her to* ALADDIN.) May you prove a worthy Queen to the greatest man in China.

(BALDROUBADOUR *and* ALADDIN *embrace.*)

(*Grand Finale.*)

CURTAIN.

www.ingramcontent.com/pod-product-compliance
Ingram Content Group UK Ltd.
Pitfield, Milton Keynes, MK11 3LW, UK
UKHW021848210426
5322IPUK00022B/533